A Northern
~ Childhood ~
GROWING UP IN OLDHAM BEFORE THE WAR

~ Audrey Evans ~

First published in 2017

This book is copyright under the Berne Convention. All rights are reserved. Apart from any fair dealing for the purpose of private study, research, criticism or review, as permitted under the Copyright Act, 1956, no part of this publication may be reproduced, stored in a retrieval system, or transmitted, in any form or by any means, electronic, electrical, chemical, mechanical, optical, photocopying, recording or otherwise, without the prior permission of the copyright owner. Enquiries should be sent to the publishers at the undermentioned address:

EMPIRE PUBLICATIONS
1 Newton Street, Manchester M1 1HW
© Audrey Evans 2017

ISBN: 978190936055-6

Mum was born and bred in Oldham and she never forgot her roots or her family.

She was an excellent mother to me and my family. I will miss her, and I'll never forget her.

Isobel Hall

CONTENTS

Acknowledgments..*8*
Beginnings *10*
Bath Times/Bed Times *15*
Come on and I'll Wash Your Head....................*17*
Father Christmas's Grotto *19*
School Days...*22*
Prize Day *24*
The Joys of Travel *30*
The Shock of War Time..................................*32*
Mr. Churchill comes to Oldham *42*
End of the War..*45*
Hollywood Comes to the Pennines......................*46*
Oldham Wakes *50*
Home Comings...*66*
Last Years at Oldham High *70*
Epilogue *74*

ACKNOWLEDGMENTS

My thanks are due to my daughter, Isobel Juliet Hall who has typed this and also made many useful suggestions. My thanks also to my grandson James Hall for using his computer skills to trace some of the more difficult references.

My thanks also to my big black and white cat, George, who knows everything and likes everything in this book.

BEGINNINGS

I was born at Greenacres Maternity Hospital on 22nd October 1929. My mother chose to go into Greenacres because she wanted to have a good address on my birth certificate. At that time we lived in West Street, a not very salubrious part of Oldham.

However the first house I remember was 233 Rochdale Rd, Oldham, known generally as Dr. Fort's surgery. It was a rather ugly house but roomy and comfortable. My grandfather and Dr. Fort had served together in World War One and there was a lot of mutual respect between them. My grandfather won the D. C. M (Distinguished Conduct medal). He had been a Sergeant Major, and then a warrant officer and Dr. Fort had been a Commissioned Officer. After the war they remained friends and both were very active members of the local St. John's Ambulance Brigade.

The hall floor at Rochdale Road had beautiful patterned mosaic tiles of blue, yellow and black. The consulting room opened on the right and in here was the all-important telephone. Dr. Fort kept in his desk a box of Oxford hard centre chocolates and would occasionally invite me to choose one and to this day I prefer hard centre chocolates. Next to the consulting room was the Dispensary, this being of special interest to me because of the lovely coloured bottles of medication. These bottles were huge and glowed red, green and blue. This was the province of Miss Whitehead, the lady dispenser, who made up the prescriptions there and then. Patients paid a few pence for their medication, which they then took home.

I much admired Miss Whitehead who was young and drove to work in a sporty little car. Women drivers were few then. She wore large leather gauntlet gloves quite unlike the dainty gloves worn by my mother and grandma. I used to sit in our living room with my legs dangling between the chair rails, turning an imaginary driving wheel to left and right, bracing my small body as I turned around hair pin bends.

One day she invited me to tea at her home near Werneth Cemetery where she lived with her parents. We had yellow jelly, something new to me. Our jelly at home was always red, and I thought that was the only colour for jelly. I

My mother and father

was fussed over and petted by Miss Whitehead's parents and then driven home, the gauntlet gloves being much in evidence, Later, I believe, Miss Whitehead married a local chemist.

We had a very big living -room which contained a small organ called a harmonium. My father played this, pumping away at the pedals and pressing down the stops above the keys. The stops had Latin names and the loud one was Vox Magna.

Then came the kitchen. A wooden rafter ran

across the kitchen ceiling and in this were three very big hooks. At Christmas time, suspended from these hooks were three Christmas puddings which were wrapped in large white cloths. One was smaller than the rest and this we ate before Christmas just to make sure that the pudding tasted good. On the floor under each pudding was a saucer into which the puddings dripped and our lovely dog, Judy, used to regularly lap up the liquid. Beyond was a small pantry and, last of all, the coal cellar, which was a mystery to me. The coalman came to the back gate and into our back yard once a month, carrying the coal bags on his shoulder and dropped the contents down the chute into the cellar. Each empty sack was spread out on the yard floor to prove that the number of bags tallied with what he charged. My grandma then gave the horse a carrot, patted his neck, paid the coalman and waved them good bye.

In the same yard near the kitchen door was a large wooden kennel made by my father. It was filled with straw and this was Judy's home. Once a year she had puppies and was a very good mother to them. When the puppies were eight weeks old my father took them to the pet shop in the centre of Oldham and received half a crown for each puppy.

BATH TIMES/BED TIMES

The routine was always the same. First my mother bathed me in the big bath which had a wooden surround. The wash bowl and lavatory pan were porcelain, with a blue floral pattern. The lavatory pan and the handle of the flush chain had the same design.

Friday night was special because I had my toe nails cut which I hated. I sat on the edge of the wooden surround while my mother carefully clipped my toe nails and flushed them down the lavatory. Then we recited:

"This little piggy went to market,

This little piggy stayed at home,

This little piggy had roast beef,

This little piggy had none

and This little piggy cried "Wee, wee, wee"

All the way home."

My mother touched each toe as we sang it. I always thought it was dreadfully unfair for the last little piggy as he got nothing. Then I went to

Me and my daughter, Isobel

bed but not before I had said my prayers. After the usual list of blessings for family members and Judy, our dog, we recited the final prayer:

"There are four angels round my bed,
One to kneel,
One to pray,
and two to carry my soul away."

I liked the two angels who knelt and prayed, but I had serious misgivings about the two angels who carried my soul. What was my soul? I reckoned it must be very heavy as it took two of them to carry it away. Perhaps they were thieves and it made me uneasy. I climbed into bed and my mother kissed me good night.

The gas light was always left on, intended to be a comfort to me. In fact, the flickering shadows on the wall kept me awake. Occasionally, during the night there would be a moment of great drama when the outside bell rang. This was always answered by my grandfather, whose heavy footsteps could be heard going down the stairs, to open the side door. If the caller was really ill my grandfather would telephone Dr. Fort. More often than not, however, we could hear him sending the person away and then calling on the stairs as he returned to bed. "Just another drunk".

COME ON AND I'LL WASH YOUR HEAD

On Friday night my hair was washed and the whole business was quite a palaver. I knelt on the rug in front of the open fire and my mother drew a lading can of hot brownish water from the side boiler. She tested it to see that it was the right temperature and I knelt down on the rug with a big bowl in front of me. Then my father took over, his big gentle hands rubbing carbolic soap into my wet hair. After a good deal of swirling his soapy hands around my hair my mother would empty the lading can to rinse it. Then my father rubbed my hair with a towel until it was nearly dry then it was my mother's turn.

She laid out several strips of material about an inch wide. I held one end of the strips in my hand and she took a length of hair and twirled it till it reached my scalp. Then twirled it down to the end of my hair and tied it in a knot. I had eight of these so-called ringlets. I slept with these ringlets which were then undone the following morning. When my mother drew them out I had eight ringlets of which I was very proud.

I always hoped for fine weather for if it rained the curl came out of the ringlets. When this happened my mother simply divided my hair into two plaits, which looked rather severe compared with the glamour of the ringlets.

FATHER CHRISTMAS'S GROTTO

Every year in early December my mother took me to visit Father Christmas in his grotto, at Lewis's, the big department store in Manchester. I enjoyed it immensely. First, we joined a long queue waiting to see Father Christmas in his grotto. Before we reached the grotto there was a small area in which we paid half a crown to receive a present. The woman at the counter asked how old I was to which my mother replied "eight years old". I listened in astonishment and whispered to my mother that I was six years old. "Yes" she said, "But you are very forward for your age and a present for a six-year-old would be too babyish for you".

At last we came to the grotto where dear old Father Christmas sat smiling at me. By his side stood the most beautiful fairy with sequins on her wings. Father Christmas indicated to me to sit on his knee and asked me my name. When I replied "Audrey" he said that it was a nice name and asked if "I was a good little girl" I looked him straight in the eye and assured him that I was a very good girl. Then he asked what I would I like for Christmas? "A Caxton printing set" I said. And he replied that he would do his best for me.

The fairy waved her magic wand over me and I tingled with delight as she waved me to the exit. There I received a present, which I was not allowed to open until Christmas day.

My mother took my hand and we went off to catch the tram back to Oldham. I was rather nervous because of the lie about my age. Would a policeman arrive on the tram to take us to prison? However as soon as we reached Werneth I relaxed because it was only three or four stops to Oldham.

In fact, the present gave me great pleasure. It was a Caxton Printing Set. It gave me joy for years to come, when I took out the little letters and stamped them on the ink pad and then on the paper.

One year, however, was fraught with anxiety for Father Christmas was wearing spectacles. Was he going blind? I wondered. However, my mother replied soothingly that it was very cold in Iceland where he lived and the spectacles kept his eyes warm. Everything was well.

There was yet another mystery about Father Christmas for King Street Stores in Oldham had a big notice in the window saying that Father Christmas was in their stores. How could it be? My mother came to the rescue again. "Father Christmas" she said "needed helpers because he couldn't be in all the stores at the same time. The one in Lewis's was the real one and all the others were his friends and helpers." Again, I could relax.

When I went to bed on Christmas Eve I always had difficulty in getting to sleep. Eventually, however, convinced I could hear the tinkle of his sleigh bells, I fell asleep.

SCHOOL DAYS

Sadly, Dr. Fort died and his practice was taken over by Dr. Law and Dr. Graham and we moved to two small terraced cottages: 10 and 26, Caroline Street, Coldhurst. There were many streets of such cottages at that time, rented by the so-called 'respectable poor'. Ours was no. 10 and my grandparents had no. 26. Our neighbours were friendly and warm-hearted and we soon became accepted by them.

It was time for me to start at Coldhurst Infant School on Bradford Street. where dear little Miss Morris was the Headmistress.

I quickly mastered the art of reading and soon found it a joy which was to last a life time. My favourite story was 'Milly Molly Mandy' of whom I never tired.

I found friends, especially Marjorie Hackney, a chatty intelligent little girl who lived opposite us in Caroline Street. Each morning I called at her house so we could walk to school together.

Both her parents worked in the cotton mill

A Northern Childhood

and Marjorie was made ready for school by her grandfather. I would watch him brush and comb her hair, single out one tress and tie a ribbon around it. It seemed a complicated matter for an elderly man and I couldn't imagine my own grandfather doing this for me.

At the age of seven I moved up into the Junior school and was taught by Mrs Wood in J1, Mrs Taylor in J2, Mr Howarth in J3, and Mrs Pownall in J4.

I had piano lessons from Miss Linda Clegg and, as none of the teachers could play the piano, I was soon asked to play a marching tune after morning assembly. I enjoyed showing off my musical ability, while everyone marched back in pairs to their classrooms.

PRIZE DAY

Prizes were given on the last day of the summer term, one for the top girl and one for the top boy, in each class. We assembled in the school hall, sitting crossed-legged on the floor and the teachers sat on chairs facing us. The hugely fat headmaster, Mr. Howarth, stood at the front and called out the names of the top girl and top boy in each class, starting with junior one.

It was my last year in Primary school and I sat expectantly listening for my name to be called out. Mr. Howarth boomed out "Top boy, Junior 4 Kenneth Whittaker" and up jumped Kenneth and stood in front of Mr. Howarth. "A sketching tablet, Kenneth" said Mr Howarth, "well done". He handed a very large pad of sketching paper to Kenneth, then shook his hand and Kenneth marched back to his place, while we applauded noisily.

"Top girl, Audrey Evans," I jumped up in front of Mr. Howarth, who shook my hand and said: "A box of pastels". I took it and scurried back to my place. I love pastilles. I took off the paper, looked in the box, and got a huge disappointment. Instead of the sugary sweets I loved were a dozen coloured pieces of chalk in a ridged box!

Worst was to come, my friend whispered "Can I have a look at them?" and grabbed the box. Out fell all the pastels and broke into bits. She was aghast and I was close to tears. Carefully, we picked up the bits and put them back in the ridges of the box. I ran home and my mother listened to my tale of woe. "It's not the prize that matters" she said, as she wiped away my tears. "You are the top girl" she said. When my father came home he was very tender as he listened to the story and we ate our tea.

Later in the evening, he said to my mother "I'm going out to get some cigarettes." He came back a few minutes later carrying a small white paper bag.

"Come on, top girl" he said and thrust in my hands a tube of Rowntree's Pastels. My mother smiled and kissed me, it hadn't been such a bad day after all.

In J4 we took what was then called the Scholarship Exam. For several years, no one had passed until Olive Shepherd passed and

Isobel and I in the garden

the following year three of us passed. When the news came, we were each given a letter to our parents and were allowed to go home early. I raced home and told my mother and then my grandparents and then my father when he came home from work. My family were hugely pleased for me and my mother wrote a letter of thanks to Mrs. Pownall for her excellent teaching.

Mrs. Pownall wore a reversible coat of fawn on one side and brown on the other. I knew no one else with such a magical garment and admired it greatly.

She and her husband lived near my aunts in Werneth. Mr. Pownall kept an Ironmongers shop and after many years he and Mrs. Pownall adopted a little boy called John.

The Scholarship meant that I had a place at Oldham High School and my life changed markedly. Life at Oldham High School was utterly different from Coldhurst School. I had to travel by bus which seemed a great adventure and I learned new school jargon.

I said "Bags me", which meant as I put my school bag on a desk, that it was mine for that lesson.

Any lateness was met with detention which involved staying in school for half an hour after lessons and writing a hundred times: "I must not be late".

A handful of pupils came from the West Riding and were allowed to leave school ten minutes early in order to catch the train, which was known locally as The Delph Donkey. It took in pupils from Delph, Diggle, Dig Lea, Denshaw and Dobcross.

In the sixth form classes were mixed, and having boys around was exciting. The staff called the boys by their surnames but the boys liked it when the girls used their first name.

Sometimes we used Shakespearian literary forms of address.

"Give thee good morrow sir." Was one such and "Fie, sir" was a term of reproof if they were too daring with us.

One day as we girls ran up the stone stairs to our form room a teacher appeared from the female staff room and one of the women teachers said "Audrey, take this letter to Mr. Smith in the male staff room". I took the letter and crossed the huge hall to the boy's side of the school. Scores of boys were racing up the steps, eyeing me with curiosity. What was a girl doing on their side of the school? I felt very scared, then a tall kindly boy who must have been a prefect, said "What are you doing here?"

"I'm looking for the male staff room, and I

don't know where it is." "Come on follow me I'll show you".

In a few minutes, we were standing outside a door marked 'Male Staff Room'. I knocked and a man came to the door and I gave him the note. Which he read quickly. "No reply," he said and disappeared inside.

Going back was easy and I walked with confidence over a sea of shiny wooden floor and delivered my message to the teacher. I scurried back to my form room and could hardly wait until break to tell the other girls that I had actually been to the boy's side of the school. What an adventure!

After my parents, my grandma and grandpa Evans were closest to me. Their affection and care for each other was rock solid. My grandpa had a horror of my grandma swallowing a fish bone. "Put on tha spectacles, Ellen" he would say watching her toy with her plate of fish. Only when the spectacles were in place would he relax and enjoy his own fish.

THE JOYS OF TRAVEL

I knew these pretty little villages quite well, for by this time my father had acquired a little Morgan. This little car gave my father great satisfaction and soon we went on family trips each weekend. There was no driving test at that time and my father simply went out with a friend who could drive who taught him basic skills.

It was a bright red three-wheeler which had two seats and a tiny one called the "dicky" which was where I sat. It had a canvass hood which was left down most of the time and closed only if it rained.

Our favourite trip was to Haydock and we drove there in our little red Morgan on the new East Lancashire road. At Haydock lived the Abbots, long-standing friends of my parents. Their house had a shared vestibule and I never tired of looking through the glass partition waving to their next-door neighbours, who always waved and smiled back.

The Abbotts had two sons, Jack and Harry, close to me in age.

Quite often we stayed overnight and I shared a bedroom with the two boys. Jack, inventive and intelligent, used to tie a piece of string around his big toe and attach it to the light switch so he could switch it on and off, to save himself getting in and out of bed.

I had my own skills for I was a regular reader of a weekly magazine which was called *Sunny Stories* written by Enid Blyton. Each week there was a competition for the best letter.

This I won and received a prize of half a crown. This was wealth indeed and a far cry from my usual Saturday penny. I then wrote a letter purporting to be from Jack and he also won half a crown, to be shared with Harry and I went up greatly in the estimation of the two boys.

Both boys went to the Grammar School in Ashton-in-Makerfield. After leaving school Harry joined the Army and Jack went on to University. Jack worked for the National Coal Board and in later years became Visiting Professor at Nottingham University. Harry sadly died in his thirties leaving a young widow and a little boy.

THE SHOCK OF WAR TIME

One Sunday morning however was very different and very sobering. It had been announced on the radio that the Prime Minister, Mr. Chamberlain, was to speak to the nation. My parents and I went to my grandparents' house. Our mood was sombre.

After his opening few sentences the Prime Minister went on to say, "Consequently, this country is now at war with Germany." I looked at the tear-filled eyes of my mother and grandma. My father and grandpa sat in stony silence.

My grandpa, born in 1872, had fought in the Boer War and in the First World War. More than most people, he knew the horrors of conflict having come through the ranks as a Sergeant Major and then a Warrant Officer. Brave as a lion, he had won the D.C.M.

We ate our Sunday lunch in subdued silence, very different from the usual happy enjoyment of roast beef and Yorkshire pudding.

A Northern Childhood

Meanwhile, day school went on much as usual. I had imagined that the German soldiers would immediately come into Oldham.

However, changes were about to come. Quite soon an air aid shelter was dug under the school playground and we were taught what to do if an air raid took place. We stood in rows with our class teacher and quickly but carefully walked down the steps into the shelter. Once we were all sitting down, the class teacher called the register. After that we had rather a jolly time. Each child was given a boiled sweet to suck and then we sang songs. My favourite was:

"We pushed the damper in

and we pulled the damper out

and the smoke went up the chimney just the same."

It was quite fun and we smiled at each other as we sucked the boiled sweets. We were encouraged to recite a poem, tell a joke, or sing a song, each followed by warm applause. I don't remember being afraid but enjoyed the whole thing. Our teachers smiled at us as we waited for the sound of the All Clear, after which, the teachers marched us back to our classrooms.

As the war progressed the air raids became more frightening.

By then I was at Oldham High School and

we were each given a gas mask. This was tested every Monday morning instead of the usual Scripture lesson. We each wore the gas mask and the form mistress would hold a piece of paper in front of the nozzle and asked us to breathe in. If the paper adhered to the mask it was working properly.

There were many jokes about our gas masks. "You look better in your gas mask," we shouted at each other. There were also fashionable carriers for the gas masks but mostly we carried them in a strong brown cardboard box with a piece of webbing over the shoulder.

My father was not called up for the armed forces because he had weak eyesight. Instead, he went to be an Engineering instructor at a Government Training College in Hounslow, Middlesex. My mother worried over him dreadfully because Hounslow was a suburb of London where there was heavy bombing. Later, however, he was transferred to a training centre at Chester to the enormous relief of my mother. Chester was a lovely walled city where there was no bombing.

Moreover, it was close enough to Oldham for us to be able to visit him regularly. Sometimes my father was able to come home for the weekend. He had digs in Philip Street, Hoole, with Mr.

and Mrs. Lowe, a childless couple. Their names were Mary and Joseph and they used to joke that they had no little baby Jesus. They made us very welcome when we came to stay with them.

At that time, Vera Lynn used to sing a song called 'That Lovely Weekend' and Mr. and Mrs. Lowe used to tease my father about it.

My special friend was Joan Howson whose father was the workhouse master. The workhouse was on Rochdale Road close to Boundary Park Hospital. Mr. and Mrs. Howson and their youngest daughter Joan lived in a cottage directly opposite the workhouse. If I went to their house early morning, I would watch with pity, the people emerging from the workhouse. Men and women, dressed in fusty garments, and looking neither to left nor right walked up Rochdale Road. All of them had the same bewildered expressions. They would have been given a good wash, a bed for the night and breakfast the next morning.

They both scared and fascinated me. Where were they going? Perhaps just to walk the streets, or sit on a park bench, or go begging from door to door.

There were plenty of beggars in Oldham, some sang in the streets, leaving a cap or hat on the cobbled streets, for passers-by to throw in pennies. My tender-hearted mother invariably gave the women singers a penny but nothing to the men. My mother used to collect money for a charity for 'Fallen Women'. I was curious to know what 'Fallen Women' were. I often fell and grazed my knees but it seemed strange that these grown-up women should do the same. My father jeered at this charity and said "These women were mainly 'tarts'." Stranger and stranger! I loved jam tarts but how could these women look like jam tarts? It was one of life's mysteries.

The side streets, like the one in which we lived, had plenty of street vendors. My favourite was the black pea man who did a roaring trade. We took our bowls into which he poured a canister of steaming hot black peas in gravy liberally sprinkled with salt and pepper. Unhygienic it may have been but they tasted delicious.

A horse drawn cart delivered milk drawn from a churn. Bessie Porter, the milk woman, came to the door where my mother waited with a milk jug and paid a penny for a gill of milk. As a great treat, Bessie, would let me ride in the cart all the way up to Godson Street.

On Sunday mornings, after church, Joan and I walked a mile or so into Chadderton to

A Northern Childhood

visit Uncle Joe and great aunt Anne Saunders who lived in a large terraced house on Garforth Street. Great aunt Anne was sister to my grandfather and a great favourite in the family. We took with us a large fatty cake which was a round piece of pastry liberally sprinkled with currents and sugar and, in return, she gave us the previous week's copy of *The Christian Herald*. This was a small black and white magazine with news of church events and one or two improving short stories which Joan and I read on the way home.

Aunt Anne had married Uncle Joe late in life, when he was a widower with two young sons. She made him an excellent wife and a good mother to his two young sons, Jim and Harold.

I always loved it when Aunt Anne visited us on family occasions. Invariably she went around to each one of us in turn, shook hands, and called out "Good morning to all". She always carried a very large handbag and there were many speculations as to what was in it. These ranged from her bank book to a pair of clean knickers.

There were two other great aunts, one always referred to as Monday aunt because that was the day she visited us. She was a tiny spinster and lived on Coppice Street. On arrival at our house, she set to work immediately polishing the cutlery. After that she would do some ironing and then dust. (Her name may be Alice?) She ate her mid-day meal, and stayed with us a short time for a chat. Then my grandma made up a parcel of food for her, gave her tuppence to cover her tram fare and off she went.

Aunty Lucy was my favourite. A tiny, smiling woman, she was my grandma's youngest sister and a widow with no children. She lived in a terraced cottage next to Failsworth railway station which seemed to shake when the trains rolled by but she loved it and in the summer often went on a cheap day return ticket to Fleetwood or Blackpool. With a few sandwiches packed for her lunch she would leave early morning and arrive home early evening, refreshed by the sun, the sea and other visitors. Aunt Lucy kept several stray cats which she loved dearly and who helped to combat what must have been her loneliness.

Years later when I was married and we lived in New Moston, I would arrive home to find her sitting on the garden wall, swinging her legs, while I made some tea for her. Despite her poverty, she never complained. She would sit on the garden swing and sing as she swung higher and higher.

At Christmas, my father used to make up a big hamper of mince pies, Christmas pudding, vegetables, chocolates, and slices of pork. After his untimely death, I continued this practice.

When I used to visit her she would always whisper, "Audrey, park your car right in front of my house" to show that her family could afford a car.

When she died, she left me her Wedgwood cups and saucers .and many happy memories.

Oldham War Memorial

MR. CHURCHILL COMES TO OLDHAM

Oldham was agog with excitement. Mr. Churchill was coming to Oldham and was due to speak from the Town Hall steps at 4.00 p.m. He had gained his first Parliamentary seat in Oldham, standing as a Liberal, although now he was a Conservative and Prime Minister.

My friend and I made a detour from our usual way home from school to stand with the huge crowd to hear him. The familiar bulky figure emerged to a huge roar of applause. His pink and white baby face broke into a smile. It was a moment to remember. He urged us to keep in good spirits, spoke of the bravery of our fighting forces and gave the familiar V sign. The crowd went mad with patriotic fervour until finally he went back into the Town Hall and the moment of history was over.

As the war progressed the air raids became more frequent. We were advised to go down to

Prime Minister Winston Churchill address crowds in his old constituency during WWII

our cellars.

As my father was an instructor at a Government Training College in Hounslow, Middlesex, my mother and I were on our own. Our kindly next door neighbours, Mr. and Mrs. Wallpole, used to invite us to stay with them in their cellar.

There was no bombing in Oldham but parts of Manchester, only seven miles away, were bombed.

From my point of view, much depended on the length of time the air raid lasted. If it went on for more than two hours we did not have to go to school in the morning but went in the afternoon.

END OF THE WAR

The war ended in Europe on V.E. Day. We had a big street party in which trestle tables were set out in the street. Everyone took some items of food. There were sandwiches, homemade buns and cakes, trifles, custard pies and jellies. It was a day to remember.

It took some months before soldiers, sailors and air men came home from the war but at least, they were safe. We were still at war with the Japanese but V.J. Day soon followed.

Uncle Samuel

HOLLYWOOD COMES TO THE PENNINES

As we grew a little older Joan and I changed the Sunday morning routine. After church, we called at our house to take Rodger, my much-loved black spaniel, for a walk. Joan, who had no pet of her own, liked to hold his lead. We called at her house and her mother gave us each a mug of steaming beef-tea, which was rich gravy which went down well.

We walked quickly to Sheep foot Lane which was on the edge of the Pennines. There was no traffic in Sheep foot Lane and we took off Rodger's lead and he frisked madly ahead of us.

We two girls then made a huge mental adjustment which took us to Hollywood! Our spirits rose in anticipation as we got ready to meet Mickey Rooney and Freddie Bartholomew. Joan ran forward first to greet Mickey and they embraced. She enquired after Judy Garland

and then the pair of them embarked on a tricky tap dance routine.

Meanwhile, I flew into the arms of Freddie Bartholomew who swirled me round in a glorious waltz. I asked after his mother whom he always referred to as "dearest" and our mood became romantic.

There we were, two little girls on the brink of adolescence, dancing our way into the future. Normality disappeared and all was fantasy. All too soon, the dream ended as we waved good bye to the two boys who disappeared from sight. In the distance, we could hear their voices promising to come back next Sunday.

Reality returned, I put Rodger on the lead and gave Joan the pleasure of walking him. We parted at her house.

Dear Joan, we remained lifelong friends. She married young, had a baby and then she and her husband emigrated to Australia. However, she made frequent visits back to England and always visited me. On her last visit, she and one of her daughters came to stay with me in Derbyshire. She was not very well and shortly afterwards her daughter wrote to tell me that she had died very peacefully after her morning swim in the sea.

"Did you have a good walk?" my mother

would ask when I returned. "See anybody I know?"

"No one at all" I replied and Rodger wagged his tail.

OLDHAM WAKES

On the Friday evening before Oldham Wakes Saturday we always went to take our leave of relatives who were staying at home. This was a prolonged business and so many last-minute reminders about taking care of our purses, sending postcards and not going into the sea on a full stomach, that it was a wonder that we ever got away at all.

One aunt was usually so affected at the thought of our venturing all the way to the Fylde coast that she would manage to let a drop a few tears as she kissed us farewell. We might have been leaving for the Far East instead of going to stay with Mrs Rigby at Fleetwood.

For me the best and totally predictable part of the evening was being given my Wakes' odd money. This stayed the same for years and I always had it totted up well in advance. Sixpence from each of my two aunts, an uncle, a grandma and two grandads, and a whole shilling from my parents, made a grand total of four shillings. Of

The population of Oldham get ready for Wakes Week

course, I always managed to put on a suitably surprised look and small wonder, for normally my sole income was a Saturday penny.

Just before we set out on Wakes Saturday morning for Werneth Station this money was placed in a small, green cotton bag tied with a long white draw tape. The whole thing was then placed around my thin young neck and dropped down the front of my dress, as it was generally held that I could not be trusted with a purse.

My mother had a similar little bag holding the hard-earned savings for our lodgings and hers disappeared in like fashion behind a genteel piece of haberdashery known as a modesty vest. At every purchase on holiday I used to haul out the little bag from the fastness of my non-existent bosom and then drop it safely back again. I rather liked it. Anyway, I was always having things hung around my neck. In winter, I had a brown Bakelite object known as iodine locket around my neck. It smelt strongly of some medicated crystals and made the other kids give me funny looks. Then, on my birthdays I had a little disc with 5, 6 or 7 on it, as the birthday might be. Once around my neck I was strictly forbidden to touch the bag until we got there. Alas for disobedience!

One terrible Wakes Saturday, as we waited

on Werneth Station, I dashed out of the waiting room in an ecstasy of delight at the sound of the approaching train, madly swinging the bag around and round on its white tape. In a trice pennies, threepenny bits, sixpences all flew merrily over the platform, railway lines and sleepers.

With recriminations voiced thick and fast, my mother salvaged what she could in her usual nimble fashion and other travellers helped. I was too appalled at what I had done to do more than stand like a frozen pillar. My father tried to rescue a particularly precariously placed sixpence but mother, afraid to lose her spouse as well as my money, called out "No, you'll be killed." And the drama ended as the train drew in.

Oh, what a terrible journey that promised to be! I knew from experience that silence was the best tactic in such circumstances. A small child huddled-up, white-faced little girl I sat, in isolation, grieving for my loss. No stockbroker at a time of falling markets ever agonised more acutely than I at that moment. I was too stunned to even count up how much had been recovered, I just knew that it wasn't all there. Eventually my mother's anger began to recede and her common sense and sympathy for me took over. Together we counted up how much capital I had left. It came to three shillings and a whole penny for the porters and regulars of Werneth Station to squander!

Even my father's offering of the corner seat, his prerogative, could not appease my misery. In hushed tones a fellow passenger asked my mother what was the matter and in equally muted tones told her. The whole compartment yearned over me. Like us, they were off on their Wakes holiday and like us had, no doubt, had to scrimp and save hard for a year to accrue enough money to have a break. Eleven pence was no joking matter. Then, such is the kindness of poor people for those in need of help, that the woman gave me a sandwich and a penny, her sister gave me two pennies, and her husband a threepenny bit! More was to come.

An elderly gentleman, seemingly aloof from the situation, felt his pocket and gruffly proffered a whole sixpence. Unbelievable! I was actually in pocket by a whole penny. It hardly seemed proper to brighten up too quickly. A decent appearance of penitence and contrition was called for, but in my heart, I gloated.

We played our usual game of who could see the sea first and we ate the cheese sandwiches and parkin that we had carried in a brown paper bag all the way from home. Our fibre suitcases, always a source of anxiety to my mother who did not trust the luggage rack, managed to withstand the journey in safety and at last we arrived at Fleetwood.

We always stayed at the same place, Mrs. Rigby's in Mowbray Road. It was a small semi-detached house with a bit of scrubby garden back and front but after our street of brick terraced cottages it seemed very grand and it had the refinement of a bathroom and indoor lavatory. Mrs. Rigby greeted us like old friends, for we went their year after year and so did my grandparents when they visited Fleetwood.

Carefully selected friends were told that we knew a "good place", but only to a chosen few was the actual address revealed lest they should usurp us when it came time for the Wakes bookings.

Mrs. Rigby could never have grown fat from the profits made on us, for we only rented a room from her. All the food we ate was taken in and each morning we shopped for vegetables, meat and carried them back for Mrs. Rigby to cook. This daily shopping was done with great care and the bag of meat chosen with rigorous accuracy. It hadn't to be so dear that it damaged our resources but not so cheap that Mrs. Rigby would be ashamed to cook it.

This nice piece of bargaining completed we could set off for the morning, my mother secure in the knowledge that Mrs. Rigby was as thrifty and careful a cook as herself and that nothing would be wasted.

Our bedroom at Fleetwood was small but at the front of the house, this being felt to be important, I had a small bed and opposite was the big bed for my parents. It also had a small chest of drawers and a wardrobe. To me the bedroom held little interest, but the dining room was another matter altogether.

The main piece of furniture in the dining room was a sideboard of which we had a half share, the other half being used by whoever rented the other bedroom, usually another small family.

In our half, we kept tea, sugar, jam, potted meat, biscuits and the like which were used at tea times. I was always agog to discover how the items in the other half compared with our own. Did they have homemade jam like ours or was it shop jam? Did they have lump sugar or was theirs the ordinary kind and did they have fancy biscuits or solar fingers?

Whenever the coast was clear I used to make a quick dash inside and, flouting every known house rule, have a quick 'rocky' as to the state of their groceries. I knew to a nicety how much salmon paste they had left and whether their digestive biscuits were running low. Had my mother known of my detective work she would have been horrified. She had constantly warned me never to touch their things. Indeed, I wasn't supposed to touch ours either. Still it was worth the danger of discovery, for the slivers of cheese and biscuit edges I purloined tasted better than they did at meal times.

In fact, meal times were somewhat strained. My table manners were held to be good and I could trot out "Please" and "Thank you" well enough. But I could not cope with the contrived conversations and tense atmosphere, which sharing a very small dining room necessitated.

At home, we talked all the time during meals of anything that interested us and this suited everybody. My mother, however, had an idea that better class families did not speak at meal times and besides, the people at the other table might be listening. As the room was so small and the tables so close that we touched elbows every time we used a knife and fork, the poor souls would have been hard put to not to listen. So, we maintained either an icy-silence or conversed on acceptable subjects in highly unnatural voices.

On Thursdays, we were given a fresh fish tea. Mr. Rigby was a trawler man and when he came home he brought fish in abundance. It was always the best meal of the week. The fish really was fresh, generously served and eaten in a spirit of great joviality because it was on the house. Anything free was welcome. It was not that we were greedy - far from it - but like thousands of other Lancashire working-class families of the Thirties, we always had to make ends meet (it was only due to the keen budgeting of my mother that we were able to have a holiday at all.) Our Wakes holidays must have been about as dull as anything one could imagine, yet to us they were bliss. Just walking on the promenade and tasting salt-spray breezes, feeling tangy air and looking at the limitless sea, made it, almost literally, another world from the factory fumes that filled the air of Oldham.

Each morning we walked in a happy trio along the sea front to The Mount which was a small green hillock surrounded by a wooden building on top of which was a big clock. No pilgrim approaching the Holy Grail did so with more reverence than my father walking up to see that clock.

It was generally reckoned in our circle

that my father knew about clocks and on most Sunday mornings at home a newspaper would be spread over the table and my father would take the clock to pieces. No surgeon felt more fervent than my father operating on the works of our ailing domestic time-pieces. The walk along the front must have been quite a trial to my mother who didn't really like walking and generally preferred "doing something useful". Never the less, walk we did.

There was no stopping for elevenses or nonsense of that kind. Indeed, I am not sure that we knew the term at that time. I would be allowed on to the sands and my parents sat on a bench sharing a newspaper. As a lot of Oldhamers were having a holiday at the same time we saw plenty of people and exchanged comments as to the merits and demerits of our lodgings.

An annual ambition of mine was to meet either Percy Pickles or Lobby Ludd in Fleetwood. These gents were employed by two leading daily newspapers and at stated times would stroll around specific areas of holiday resorts waiting to be recognised by predatory holiday makers. Once discovered they rewarded the challenger with a five-pound note, providing they could come out with the required spiel which went:

"You are Percy Pickles. I am a regular reader of the *Daily Dispatch* and I claim the reward." I was bent on finding one of these pimpernel-like creatures and every morning I intently studied the newspaper pictures of them. They were always cunningly posed so that only a half-face or profile partly-hidden by a hat, was revealed.

I dreamed joyfully of the triumph of handing my mother a whole five-pound note. Could we, I wondered, stay on for another week, if I could boost our finances in this way? So, once on my own, having promised to be back at Mrs. Rigby's house by one o'clock sharp, I would hare along the promenade accosting innocent gentlemen in trilby hats, or scan the profiles of the few struggling fishermen at the end of the pier, lift white handkerchiefs from the faces of snoozers on the sands, addressing each and every one as Percy Pickles or Lobby Ludd.

Of course, they all gave me a smart brush-off but I was not easily daunted and the morning would pass away, happily enough, if not exactly profitably. When I didn't find them, I was sure that they must have forgotten to turn up. Yet next day there would be a newspaper of a smiling winner waving a five-pound note in her hand. How had I slipped up? It remained an unsolved mystery.

A big event came near the end of our holiday when we bought presents for the family members at home. To this end, I always set aside a shilling of my own money. I needed a penny each for my two aunts, an uncle, two grandads, one grandma and threepence each for my parents. This was a fair cut out of my small hoard but I never grudged it. It was expected of me and it taught me the very real pleasure of giving.

For the men, I would select a pencil with a rubber on the end, a jotter, or a very small cigar. It was important that my aunts and grandma should all have the same thing. Colour could vary but not the item itself. So, I would choose, with infinite discrimination, a blue comb for one aunt, a pink one for the other and a yellow one for my grandma. (My grandma was my favourite and so I gave her the colour I liked best.) For a penny, I could choose from an array of broaches, combs, tea-caddy spoons, nail files or hankies. With such a choice, it was hard to decide and I had to be careful not to duplicate last year's gifts.

My mother was easy to please because she would go with me and choose something she liked, costing no more than the prescribed threepence. A string of beads, three egg-cups, or a little bottle of scented water were all within my means and her genuine pleasure at the small gift was ample reward.

My father was given the morning off while we went on this important business. Men in our family weren't expected to know about present buying and he affected to scorn the whole business. We considered him superfluous on these occasions so he would wander off, happy no doubt to be relived of our non-stop chatter. Mostly he went to watch the ferry come in from Knott End, or to have another look at the Mount Clock.

We all loved going to Knott End. Crossing the strip of grey, oily water on the ferry boat was to me as exciting as a voyage on an ocean-going liner. In the few minutes it took us to cross, I had skipped right around the deck, tumbled down the steps into the cosy, beery-smelling cabin, and nosed into the engine room to be sent out sharpish. I always pestered my father to make sure we were the first to get on and the last to get off, so that we had the longest ride in terms of time.

On these voyages, my mother was always coy and fluttery as she held herself to be a poor sailor and I was hard put to curb my impatience. However, her suffering did have a rewarding aspect from my point of view, because it meant that we should stop at the small café at the top of the little quayside and be revived with a cup of tea. The wild expense of this was justified by the certain knowledge that my mother would surely collapse unless refreshed in this way.

We used to look at a house called Quail View as we walked into Knott End. It was a perfectly ordinary house but the name intrigued us and, in fact, some years later we spent a holiday there. We would walk in the direction of Preesall and my father and I would play catchers with a tennis ball. My holiday sandals of light-brown leather set me skipping and jumping in a far more uninhabited way than my customary sensible school shoes allowed but both my parents must have looked quite dressy in their holiday togs.

Being at work for my father often meant being dirty, so I expect he felt like a gentleman in his flannels, brown shoes and sports jacket. In fact, he was more of a natural gentleman than anyone I ever knew.

Wakes week also meant a week of late nights for me. At home bed time was seven o'clock, with no remission except for Mondays, when I was allowed to stay up late to listen to" Monday Night at Seven o'clock" on the wireless. When this programme changed to "Monday Night at Eight o'clock" it was a small calamity for me, as I loved the adventures of Inspector Hornpipe and his "deliberate mistake" and was denied this pleasure as it was felt that eight o'clock was too late a bed time for a little girl.

On holiday, however, I accompanied my parents to places of light entertainment. We patronised the Follies, the Pier Review, the bowling green and the band concerts. Some of the Follies were really quite awful and even at that age I realised that the lady with all the yellow hair and the foreign-looking man who held her hand, could not sing. However, it never detracted from my whole-hearted enjoyment of the show, especially the zany tap-dancers and the conjurer and the comic who told jokes I wasn't supposed to understand.

On our last night we went out for our final treat. For this we went to a fish and chip restaurant and had plaice, chips, peas, brown and white bread and a pot of tea. An often-stated maxim of my mother was that "You can always rely on Fleetwood fish" so we knew in advance we were going to enjoy it, as it had her personal seal of approval and enjoy it we did!

Going home was a silent business. Mrs Rigby would kiss all three of us and assure us that she would keep a place for the following year but I still hated leaving Fleetwood. The journey back seemed short, uneventful and drab. After such superior placenames as Squire's Gate, Thornton and Cleveleys, Werneth sounded ordinary to say the least. Still, my grandma and grandad would have a big high tea waiting for us and there were many loving embraces all round and exclamations of wonder that we had managed to reach home safely. We had not been robbed by pick-pockets, victimised by sharp practice, fallen over board from the Knott End ferry, nor had our finger ends caught in the train doors. Such pitfalls were as real to us as yellow fever and hostile natives might be to the African explorer.

In the evening, my aunts and uncle would come around to greet us and there would be more kisses all round, for what we lacked in money we made up for in real affection and loving concern. I would proffer my largesse of combs, tie-pins and the like and to my gratification each recipient would declare it to be "just what I wanted." For days afterwards those of us who had been away would lord it over the other kids in the street, especially the luckless ones who had never even seen the sea (heaven knows there were enough of them in those days.) We would swap stories comparing the delights and relative merits of Blackpool, Fleetwood, Morecambe and Cleveleys. No one in our street was adventurous enough to even consider the south coast. For us it did not exist!

I had one adjective for Fleetwood that always floored everyone else. It was "select" because my mother had a little holiday booklet describing it thus and who could deny the printed word.

So, no matter what the claims of other kids as to the charms of their boarding houses, I absolutely knew that Mrs. Rigby's at Fleetwood was *the* best place to go for a holiday. Hadn't my mother said so?

HOME COMINGS

Among the most potent of my childhood memories are of being at home with my mother and father. In winter, once school was over, it soon grew too dark to play outside. I used to beg my mother to let me have a friend in for company. Our house was so small that the only possible place was under the big square table in the living room. With the folds of the dark heavy chenille table cloth hanging to the ground in a dignified order it made a splendid private den.

We would fold newspapers into fans, or squabble amicably over a game of Snap, played with a set of Cow and Gate cards.

Sometimes we read each other's palms, making the prognosis rosy or frightening according to our moods.

Like all the other women, my mother liked to have the meal absolutely ready for when my father came home. This was a point of honour as a worker wasn't supposed to be kept waiting for his tea. Succulent odours of hot-pot, meat puddings or pie would permeate the tiny cottage tantalisingly.

Some of the women stood at their front doors, wearing clean pinnies and mobcaps to show that the house work was over for the day and as a signal they were ready for a chat with their neighbour.

On Fridays, each house boasted a newly-mopped front. This meant that the paving stones in front of the door and under the window had been washed and then stoned with a donkey stone or a bit of yellow stone.

Mopping the front was a ritualistic weekly event and my mother used to whiten the edge of the step and window-sill with a white stone as a kind of aesthetic gesture to round off the business.

We never bought the stones. The rag-and-bone man gave them to us in exchange for old rags.

On very cold evenings we would sit on the rug in front of the fire, forsaking the cosy gloom of the table's sheltering cover exchanging for a chance to "tell shapes", which were conjured up from the patterns made by the coals in the fire.

The black-leaded range was an impressive affair and from it we heated the water in the side boiler. It warmed the oven in which all our food was cooked, toasted bread in front of the open coals, dried our hair on Friday nights and stood the clothes maiden in front on wet wash-days.

Two brass horses gleamed proudly on either side of the hearth and numerous bits of Goss china, brought back from the seaside holidays, were set along the mantelpiece.

Just before my father was due to arrive; mother would put up the blower to get the coal dancing into energetic crazy flames giving out small vicious sulphurous spits every now and then.

Watching "for't gas lighter" was an evening pleasure. Just before dusk a thin, jacketed and capped man used to walk around the Coldhurst area and light the street lamp at the corner opposite our house. With his long pole the gas lighter would open the little door of the lantern at the top of the lamp stand and light the gas.

At first it would struggle to shine and then give out a cheerful, steady, pale yellow light. On wet nights, it was enhanced a thousand-fold with reflections in myriads pelting rain drops beating on the glass panes.

I loved that lamp. It was in turn a "barley ground" in street games, or a counting place, or sometimes I would throw my skipping rope over its arm and have a chair ride. Once a big boy tied me to it until I yelled to be set free, but I wasn't daunted.

When the street lamps were being taken away in the sixties an old neighbour of ours, who still lived there, wrote to tell me and I bought "our lamp" from Oldham Corporation. It has followed me from New Mills, to Ashford in the Water, Darley Dale and Littleover, still giving me great pleasure.

My son-in-law always refers to it as "Big Oldham" and has promised me that when I die it will have a home with him and my daughter and their children.

LAST YEARS AT OLDHAM HIGH

The six years I spent at Oldham High School were, on the whole, profitable. Most of the teachers were women because the male teachers had been called up to join the fighting forces.

I thoroughly enjoyed the sixth form where the classes were mixed. The boys brought vigour and fun into lessons and we would pretend to be characters from Shakespeare and say "Give thee good morrow kind sir." and the boys would make a mock bow. A boy called Stewart Long was one of the funniest and would often stand on top of his desk to address us.

Our teachers called the boys by their surnames which was quite a novelty to us girls. It was time for us to choose where to go after we left school and Manchester University, Leeds University, and the Teaching Training Colleges, were very popular. At school, we were interviewed for places at college or university.

My first choice was Bingley Teacher Training

College, a grade A college and one of the best in the country. Some weeks after my interview a letter arrived saying that I had gained a place there. I was delighted as my school days were at an end.

Bingley is a small town in the Aire Valley. Midway between Bradford and Keighley. The college itself was up a very steep hill, a mile or so away from the little town and each of the halls of residence were named after a famous Yorkshire man or woman, namely, Acland, Priestly, Ascham, Hild and Alcuin. I had been assigned to Acland.

The college made every effort to make the students feel at home and I received a letter a few weeks before my arrival from a student named Dorothy Moffat who came from Whalley Range in Manchester. She wrote to say that she would be my college mother. All students became part of a so-called family. Dorothy's roommate, Julia, would be my aunt. The other student who would be sharing my room would be my sister, and her name was Margaret Brown.

Other girls in our family were, Rita Needle from Sheffield and Helen Roberts from Lincoln. My so-called aunts were called Mabel Brown. Mab Brown was one of the prettiest girls I had ever met. Her father was a clergyman and if

My husband and I

anyone did any small kindness to her she would say "bless you". She had a boyfriend training to be a Doctor in Edinburgh and they wrote to each other every day.

The Warden of the college was a no nonsense woman with a magnificent bosom. She was Miss McCleod. There were strict rules about visitors. Boyfriends had to be out of our rooms by 7p.m.

Our evening meal was at 6.p.m. and we sat

at a family table. We lined up at a hatch to get our meals but there were rules regarding this. One had to ask another girl if you wanted any more food and the other girl replied yes or no and would go to the hatch to receive the extra food.

I was due to share a room with a girl called Margret Brown, but she did not arrive until two weeks later because she had been ill with Meningitis.

Margaret's background was utterly different from my back ground. She came from Skegness, a small seaside town and her parents were divorced. Her elder brother Jack had been in the Air Force, but was reported "missing presumed dead".

Margaret was devoted to her mother who was Welsh and always referred to as Mi.

We remained friends for many years after college until one year I received no Christmas card from her. She had set off for school on the first day of term, her car had skidded on black ice and her back was broken. After many months in hospital she had to stand up in a walking frame and although we still corresponded it eventually stopped.

Sharing a room required give and take between students e.g. Margaret could not stand my clock ticking while she was studying, so I put it in my drawer. In return, she used to set my hair after its Friday night shampoo.

The two years at Bingley were the happiest of my life.

EPILOGUE

In our family was a very small man named John Evans, he was a cousin of my grandfather. He was always known in the family as 'Little Jack'. He was a bit of a loner but every now and again he would come to visit us.

We did not hear from him for some time but he had been to America and returned with a large gold nugget. This gold nugget he presented to the Royal Family and in return a street was named after him.

Quite recently I rang Oldham Borough Council to discover if the street was still there. It is indeed! It is next to Henshaw Street and on the other side it leads to Oldham Market.

Jack must have been quite a remarkable man.

Printed in Poland
by Amazon Fulfillment
Poland Sp. z o.o., Wrocław

25075982R00043